My Heart chooses For me

Written by Vanessa Concepcion-Limage

ISBN:979-8-9854817-5-4
Copyrights by Vanessa concepcion

Table of Context

Introduction ....PG 3
Our Eyes Locked ....PG 4
Third Floor...PG 8
It's who i am...PG 10
Our Bench...PG 12
Our first date ....PG 14
Official..PG 17
A Nutriment & a Rose..PG 19
Love Will Bring Us Back Together…..........................PG 21
Lust Broke usr..PG 24
Accountability..PG 26
The next step...PG 28
Our first home..PG 30
Our Boys...PG 33
A anniversary to remember…....................................PG 35
A thank you to my readers..PG 38

Introduction

Hello, my readers,

This is my first book about my feelings, yet my heart has been a writer since I was 10. I have been through a lot especially when it came to my heart. I held my emotions and kept my heart inside a box but as time went by i opened it up Because of love. I am now showing you my pain; happiness and confusion of my heart versus my mind.

I want to thank everyone who gave me a reason to write. Pouring my heart out is harder than it seems. Thank you to those who knew how good I was and supported me through it all. One more special thank you is to my husband(Ron), who without him I would not know what love is.

<u>Our eyes locked</u>

We locked eyes when we first met, It felt as if the whole

world stood still that morning, and yet,

It also felt as if i had taken a pill Of reality,

When I heard you were talking to someone who was not me.

I could tell when you spoke about her, she was your first.
Can I say love or can I just say interest?
Did She love you, like I could have?
Maybe you just thought that love, but I think she is your past. I am here now, I can love you in the present.
But who am I kidding, I dressed like a boy and acted like a blonde. He was not mine so instead I said It was just a lie that liking him at all was in my head.
I also told myself he was just Something to distract me as i was
trying to dream my work shift away. We were In a crowded area like a flock of birds(Pages) in a park.
While I just stared at you.
Not noticing the trance I was in.
When I felt myself staring I paused,
turned away like I didn't even care. Like I didn't need a cause to even be there Or I didn't even need you to notice me. Another lie I told myself.
But then you got closer, and I felt like a teenage girl Who had a cause to stay to get to know you better,
To see if you were worth exploring.
I noticed you were liked by many, So once again in my head giving up the fight that you didn't even know I was having. Then I heard your voice asked
"Do you need my help?",

Turn around to see your face again locking eyes.
My voice wanted to say yes instead I just yelped.
You helped me while I blushed.

.

You asked me my name and I froze looking confused. Why was this such a hard question?
I wanted to hit myself. Just tell him!
Before you know it, your true love appeared once again in our conversation. OUR conversation!
I wanted to scream "Who cares!" but I didn't
But before you disappeared back into the crowd you turned and looked at me and waved Goodbye. As if we were friends for years.
I felt our locked eyes once again but longer this time.
You made my first day worth staying, even if you were just doing your job.

The third floor

I met you once, and it only took a second to make my heart

skip a beat.

I saw your smile and i wanted to seek

Your life, see if i could find a way in.

Into your eyes or at least your space.

learn to become your one and true sin.

The third floor is where we worked as one.

We laughed, worked hard and yet had fun.

We talked about family and how they drove us up the walls.

Yet no matter how close we were,

I still felt that wall of emotions you had so tall.

You were still half empty cup of water, come you can't hold it all.

But i feel the need to want to stay on that third floor

Because I was close enough to be near you and one day it will fall.

All of a sudden my heart just drops,

You broke your wall but It wasn't for me,

I couldn't understand."Why, it couldn't be me?"

My feelings were staring at you so I had to leave. I left and went to live a new life. I Decided to move on.

In my heart and mind i still saw your smile felt your connection,

Like an old song. Called "The third floor."

It's Who i am

I am weird, I fall too fast,

I am goofy,

I always have to have the last,

Word.

Some of my words are Slurred.

I hold in my feelings,

Until they bust out like

A storm out of nowhere,

Wanting to tear down the houses

Of my emotions. I do before i think,

I leave dishes in my sink,

until the next day.

But my heart is full Of love,

That can not be touched,

And in loving anyone as much as i do

I really don't ask for much.

So what i am saying is love me,

Because this is who i am and i can't change,

I won't change. It's who I am.

Our Bench

Our lunches were one of the greatest things i remember

We were out on that bench forever

Sharing pizza slices like it was our last meal.

You made me more than feel as though we were the only people there

It was so unreal. But everyday we made sure it was our time to be alone and be on our own.No family,no friends no, coworkers lurking.

Just me, you, the pizza slice and soda we are slurping on. At first we were just friends laughing our stories away,then as we got closer I felt the waves turn from liking you to loving you and it was just so great,the memories of the Bench will never go away,our kids will know this bench and make their own memories on our Bench.

<u>*Our first date*</u>

I got dressed in an outfit that I never thought I would wear. It was a pencil beige shirt, a not so silky but close enough blouse with white and beige stripes. With my flat longhair. I had wedges that made me become 4 '11 to 5' 1 and for the first time I felt like I was someone. I had this straw hat that brung the outfit all together and had to hold it down sometimes because of the weather.

You had slacks on, dark beige, cream shirt, glasses on that made you look like Wanya. From boys to men if you have a clue look it up on google.

Here I go again falling for you. We have been together a billion times but this time it was more different .My hands were clamming and you made me blush.

What is this feeling I have, it's too much. I never thought I would find someone who understood but you were the one like the one who said you could. We went to the movies and as we sat in the dark I wanted you to kiss me but my body became too hot. Not even half of the movie was done.

It was just beginning to be fun, my mom called me time to go home. How embarrassed I was, my date was about to end but he took me all the way home before he left.

We kissed. I don't care that my date ended because this is all I wanted as soon as I saw him. Our first date was a day i will not forget and I can't wait until the next one and see what happens next.

Official

We have been together so many times,but a question remained.Where do we stand, do we get a name? What do I mean by a name you say? Are we actually a couple or do we just hang? I asked him.I needed to know where to go.He thought we were who i wanted us to be but he didn't even ask me. So he made it a date and as we sat in our diner spot in our favorite seat near the window. He Finally asked me, " Would you like to be my girlfriend." Of course I said "YES"! It wasn't a marriage proposal but I feel like it's the best.
For now,But we are now official and we are all good,
Let's take the time to say I knew he could be the man that I need in my life. One day I will officially one day maybe be his wife.

A Nutriment & a Rose

I have had many feelings before but this feeling was extra strong. I hoped and prayed that I was wrong, but the stick was pink and it was strong. I am only in my 20's and i freaked out,what am i gonna do now? I started overthinking in my head. "I just began to live. I don't have money or time to focus on anything else. My whole life I didn't get to focus on me .Why now?" I showed the pink to him and he smiled as I cried on the floor. I needed a moment and he left out the door

because I couldn't be consoled. No matter what he said I just freaked out. How can he be so happy? While I'm in doubt. Then a few moments later after i was almost done with my crying he walks in and there was no denying,

He handed me a nutriment and rose and said "I got you and it will be okay" Why did I believe him? All I can do is smile and say,in my head. I guess if i had to have a baby no better than him because he was my love and i believed what he said.

Love Will Bring Us Back Together

You were on my mind. We have been separated for awhile now and I must say I missed you. I wondered if you had someone new. I wondered if you even thought of me. I wondered if you were at the place where we met. I decided I should go and see and not ask questions. Back to the library I directed my way and hoped for the best.

My luck you weren't there so i let my feelings go. I guess this was the end of our show. Why did I even think he would be in this world, waiting for me like some helpless girl?
But then I heard he went to my old jobs as well to find what I left behind but new directions lead me to new hell.

I can't believe we missed each other more times that I can tell. Some how i got your number and I decided to call.

I was sweating and my heart was bouncing off the wall.
You answered me and I was just in shock.

I said "Hello" and asked if he knew who I was. Of course he knew me but I wanted to see if he still remembered my voice but the racing in my heart didn't stop.

Before you know it we will be talking again. We went further because we became friends then our story started again and love will bring us back together at the end.

Lust Broke us

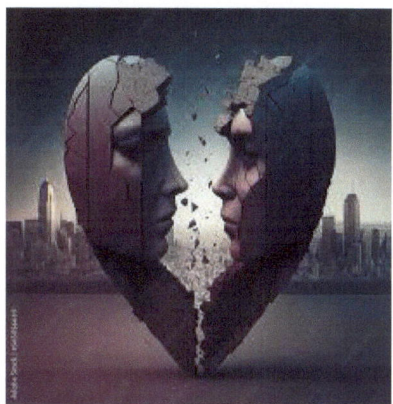

I guess I should have known that no one is perfect. We both looked outside our circle. We both thought it was worth it.

We found eachother out and trust me it hurt, but lust is an evil thing and it has its kind of sin.
We both thought we could handle what was about to come but boy we didn't know it would get to us choosing and who from.
Lust is stronger in your mind, confusing lust for love no matter our time.
Yet you couldn't choose, I walked away but it hurt me so much no man was the same to me and my heart had no trust. No man was you and lust broke us up.

She wasn't brand new. Lust you had to win and show your strength but hopefully he will chase me because fake love will end.

<u>Accountability</u>

We both messed up and messed up badly. Sometimes we end up sad, sometimes we argue badly.

Who would have known there was another pink stick showing, in my belly another baby was growing.

Yet it wasn't yours but the person it was not a father or anything more to me, it didn't seem to bother you which meant more to me.

I let him go and I wanted us back eventually. I know we now have our own lives stacked but think about a matter of fact, you wanted me too despite this baby. The back and forth did drive us a bit crazy. Somehow you were just ready to be the man I needed lately.

You took on my broken heart and didn't fall apart. We both took our past year in accountability and made us one.

Then you took on my responsibility that made us come together like a family that was on a tv show who had parents and kids living the dream who would have known.

We accounted for our past mistakes.

Accountability is what made us last and our love wasn't fake.

We both definitely learned from our past.

To be better and talk it out, this is what love is all about.

The next step

The next step was, as you can see, it's time to marry us with glee. Very few come to witness our love that consumed us with happiness. He had me and I had him, that was enough. Our family of four was everything a mother can ask for.

I was so nervous I remember asking " Are you sure you want to marry me?"

He was sure and he made me sure that this was the right choice. You can even see the happiness from our boys.

Love brought us to this step, can't wait to see what's next.

Our First Home

We left New York because of covid and it was getting worse out there so making the move was worth it. We got our first home in another state. I was beyond happy, I must say. It was a lot to get used to and we also had our first car.

Traveling to a store was close but if you were walking it was far. The area was clean and quiet made us feel like this was it. It was what we needed to feel calm enough again to enjoy our life.

My kids were safe and I felt like an appreciative wife.
I know it was hard for my husband because he still works in New York but he got used to it despite what toll it took. He was a great husband and father if you took a look, on how far we got and how our past had its own book. This life was for us even if our past was hard.

My house was awesome even though it didn't have a backyard. He feels more at home when he comes from the city because all the craziness NYC is always busy. He was happy to come home to a nice calm area. Less traffic and a sense of relaxation and NYC was full of hysteria.

There is no other feeling than the Realization that this is our home and it feels like a permanent vacation and we're together as a family not on our own.

Our boys

Oh, how our children have grown. We did not know everything about being parents but we learned dipsite of the unknown. One is in college as the other is learning to be a preteen. It's a big roller coaster. I know the parents know what we mean.

You and I did surprisingly well as parents and because our boys have great hearts and a lot of talents. They made us complete as soon as they were born.

They were meant for us and I say from great beyond. They are younger versions of us all the good and the bad but their minds are their own and that is something that made me glad. They are brighter than many kids I know. I see their future being bright as far as the sun will go. When they become men as time goes by, me and my husband should be proud of each other because Dna does not lie. Seeing them grow up might make us cry.

To our boys you were worth every moment in time.

An anniversary to remember

It started in a bar drinking on a weekend, you finally had off and i was freaking,with happiness.

It was a karaoke night that apparently, you got more attention than I did. Because you sang a song they loved and I felt defeated. We talked about our 10th anniversary coming up and you refilled our cups with great drinks. My sister was there so it was a fun night because we love when we get to link. I know something about hanging with a sister makes drinking a little better. The air was good and the day had great weather.We had all sought ideas and we talked about them together.

We thought about bars and dinners,talked about parties and you decided to leave the table and let's just say it went from a party to a Renewal of our wedding.

We started putting all the pieces together and the ideas were spreading. You were surprised at first but then agreed it's a good idea this time we had everything we needed, everything we ever wanted here. We were married and already had two kids.

We lived in a great home, we had two cars to travel and we had more than enough.
The walk down the aisle was in our home as I saw you smiling.

I noticed the people around us were not alone. Our friends and family were there, not like before and it was a dream come true for a woman to marry the man you really loved and adored.

Our anniversary was something to remember because we as a family did all of it all together. I will marry you a billion times over despite the weather.

Thank you readers!

I am so happy I can share this journey with you. I hope you have your own happiness. Through my journey I learned a lot that there is real love out there. The grass is not always greener on the other side and you can have anything good in your life if you are willing to fight for it.

Thanks for joining me on this journey.

www.ingramcontent.com/pod-product-compliance
Lightning Source LLC
Chambersburg PA
CBHW041745040426
42444CB00004B/181